West Chicago Public Library District
118 West Washington
West Chicago, IL 60185-2803
Phone # (630) 231-1552

A T. REX NAMED SUE

Sue Hendrickson's Huge Discovery

by Natalie Lunis

Consultant: Philip J. Currie, Ph.D.
FRSC, University of Alberta

BEARPORT
PUBLISHING

New York, New York

Credits

Cover, © Charles McGrady Studio; Title Page, © The Field Museum, Neg# GN89860_7C; 4, © Ira Block / National Geographic; 5, © Black Hills Institute of Geological Research, Inc.; 6, © Francois Gohier / Photo Researchers, Inc.; 7, © Black Hills Institute of Geological Research, Inc.; 8, © Black Hills Institute of Geological Research, Inc.; 10–11, © Karen Carr; 12, Kathrin Ayer; 13, © Black Hills Institute of Geological Research, Inc.; 14, © Black Hills Institute of Geological Research, Inc.; 15, © Ira Block / National Geographic; 16, © Black Hills Institute of Geological Research, Inc.; 17, © Black Hills Institute of Geological Research, Inc.; 18, © Louie Psihoyos / Science Faction; 19, © Black Hills Institute of Geological Research, Inc.; 20, © Rick Maiman / Corbis Sygma; 21, © 2006 Ferorelli; 22T, © The Field Museum; Neg# GN88584_10c; 22B, © The Field Museum; Neg# GN88863_15c; 23, © Ira Block, National Geographic; 24, © Tannen Maury / The Image Works; 25, © Reuters / Corbis; 26, © Ira Block / National Geographic; 27, © AFP / Getty Images; 28–29, Rodica Prato; 28, Kathrin Ayer; 29T, © Natural History Museum Picture Library, London; 29B, © Luis Rey.

Publisher: Kenn Goin
Editorial Director: Adam Siegel
Creative Director: Spencer Brinker
Photo Researcher: Beaura Kathy Ringrose
Design: Dawn Beard Creative

Special thanks to Larry Shaffer at the Black Hills Institute of Geological Research, Inc.

Library of Congress Cataloging-in-Publication Data
Lunis, Natalie.
  A T. rex named Sue : Sue Hendrickson's huge discovery / by Natalie Lunis.
      p. cm. — (Fossil hunters)
  Includes bibliographical references and index.
  ISBN-13: 978-1-59716-259-3 (lib. bdg.)
  ISBN-10: 1-59716-259-0 (lib. bdg.)
  ISBN-13: 978-1-59716-287-6 (pbk.)
  ISBN-10: 1-59716-287-6 (pbk.)
  1. Sue (Tyrannosaurus rex)—Juvenile literature. 2. Tyrannosaurus rex—South Dakota—Juvenile literature. 3. Hendrickson, Sue, 1949- —Juvenile literature. I. Title. II. Series.

  QE862.S3L86 2007
  567.912'9—dc22

                              2006005858

For more information, write to Bearport Publishing Company, Inc., 101 Fifth Avenue, Suite 6R, New York, New York 10003. Printed in the United States of America.

10 9 8 7 6 5 4 3 2 1

Table of Contents

One Last Look

Susan Hendrickson searched the dry, rocky ground below the cliff. She knew she didn't have much time. The other members of her team had gone into town to get a tire fixed. Soon they would be back at camp, getting ready to leave South Dakota's **badlands**. The summer was ending, and so was the team's hunt for dinosaur **fossils**.

Susan Hendrickson in South Dakota's badlands

After only a few minutes, Susan spotted some brown pieces of bone at her feet. Then she looked up. Several large bones were sticking out of the cliff. Susan climbed up to get a closer look.

"Wow," she said to herself.

North America's badlands are full of rocks that have been shaped by harsh winds. In some places these lands look like the surface of the moon.

Fossil hunters use clues from the bones they find to learn what **extinct** animals, such as dinosaurs, looked like, how they moved, and where they lived.

A Fossil Hunter Named Sue

One adventure always seemed to lead to another in Susan Hendrickson's life. By the time she was 20 years old, she had become an expert diver. During a diving trip to the Dominican Republic, she visited the mountains. She saw a piece of **amber** there. Inside was an insect. It was millions of years old, yet perfectly **preserved**.

The insect trapped inside this amber is 45 million years old.

A piece of amber is tree **sap** that hardened and became stone millions of years ago. Sometimes an insect became trapped in it while it was still a sticky liquid.

Susan read all about amber, insects, and **ancient** life. She became an expert on fossils and was invited to join a **dig** in Peru. There she met another fossil hunter. He asked her to join a new dig—this time in the badlands of South Dakota.

Susan and other fossil hunters found this whale skeleton while searching the Atacama Desert in Peru.

The Bones in the Cliff

On August 12, 1990, Susan steadied herself on the cliff in South Dakota. She looked carefully at the bones. She could see they belonged to a huge dinosaur. The bones were hollow. Among large dinosaurs, only meat-eaters had hollow bones.

Susan put the facts together. The only huge meat-eater known to have lived in this area was *Tyrannosaurus rex* (ti-*ran*-uh-SOR-uhss REKS).

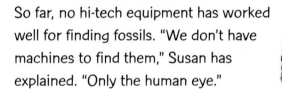

So far, no hi-tech equipment has worked well for finding fossils. "We don't have machines to find them," Susan has explained. "Only the human eye."

Susan at the spot in South Dakota's badlands where she found the dinosaur bones in the cliff

Susan couldn't wait to tell the others. After all, only ten *Tyrannosaurus rex* (*T. rex*) skeletons had ever been found. Almost all of them were missing many bones. Could this new find turn out to be as huge as it seemed?

Where *T. rex* Lived

Alberta

Saskatchewan

Manitoba

Ontario

Montana

North Dakota

Minnesota

Idaho

South Dakota

Wyoming

Nebraska

Utah

Colorado

Kansas

CANADA

UNITED STATES

- ● Some of the places where *T. rex* has been found
- ● Place where Susan's *T. rex* was found

Dinosaurs lived in every part of the world, but *T. rex* bones have been found only in western North America.

The Tyrant Lizard King

Tyrannosaurus rex skeletons were first found in the early 1900s. At that time, scientists gave the dinosaur its name, which means "**tyrant** lizard king." Today scientists still think that *T. rex* ruled as the largest and **fiercest** meat-eating dinosaur of its time.

T. rex was about 40 feet (12 m) long and 15 feet (4 m) high at the hips. Its size is often compared to a school bus.

T. rex's sharp, curved teeth were the size of bananas. They helped *T. rex* rip into the flesh of the dinosaurs it ate. The monstrous meat-eater's jaws were powerful enough to crush its victim's bones.

T. rex lived around 67 to 65 million years ago, near the end of the time of the dinosaurs.

A Dinosaur Graveyard

The badlands of South Dakota are one of Earth's great dinosaur **graveyards**. Fossil hunters search the cliffs because they are like rocky **tombs**. Dinosaur bones have been buried there for millions of years.

From Dinosaur to Fossil

1 A *Tyrannosaurus rex* dies.

2 The animal's soft parts, such as its flesh and eyes, rot away. Its hard parts, such as teeth and bones, are left.

3 Layers of sand and mud cover the bones and teeth. Minerals in water seep into the bones and teeth and fill all of the tiny spaces in them.

Very few of the dinosaurs that lived long ago became fossils, however. If a dead dinosaur didn't get buried quickly, it would rot away. The *T. rex* that Susan Hendrickson found must have been buried suddenly—perhaps during a flood. Otherwise, its bones would not have been preserved until that summer day in 1990.

④ The bones and teeth survive as fossils for millions of years.

Dinosaur bones that become fossils are usually covered with sand or mud. Over millions of years, the sand or mud changes to rock.

A *T. rex* Named Sue

When Susan's team saw what she had found, they were as excited as she was. They agreed that the bones belonged to a *T. rex*. The team decided to name the giant animal after its discoverer. From that day on, the dinosaur was known as Sue.

Using only simple tools, Susan and the rest of the crew cleared away the huge amount of rock that lay on top of the bones.

The next day, the fossil hunters got to work. Their first step was to remove 30 feet (9 m) of rock from the cliff. They couldn't use heavy machines because the **fragile** fossils might get damaged. Instead, the team used shovels, crowbars, and picks to reach the bones. Once they did, they were amazed by what they saw.

Susan and her coworkers had no way of knowing if their *T. rex* was male or female. Today, scientists are trying to find ways to identify a dinosaur's **gender** by looking at its skeleton.

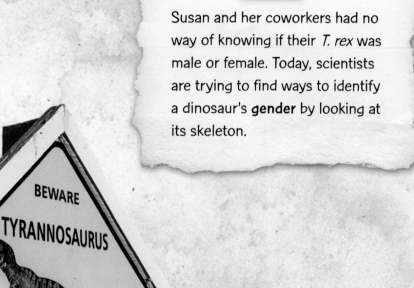

BEWARE
TYRANNOSAURUS

AHEAD

Fossil hunters put this sign up for fun in the area where Sue was discovered.

15

Sue Is Unearthed

The team uncovered more and more bones. They couldn't believe their luck. Sue was the largest and most complete *T. rex* ever found. "She just kept getting better and better. We were all in such shock," Susan recalled.

Fossil hunters Susan Hendrickson, Peter Larson, and Susan's dog, Gypsy, pose with the skull.

For 17 days, the fossil hunters dug up the bones. They left a layer of rock around each one to protect it. They also covered the blocks of rock with layers of **burlap** and **plaster**. Now the fossils could be safely loaded onto trucks.

At last, Susan and the others left the badlands, still happy and excited. They were looking forward to seeing Sue's skeleton put back together. Yet they were in for another shock.

The team covered this rock with layers of burlap and plaster to protect Sue's bones, which were inside.

Recording information is an important part of fossil hunting. The team took many photos to show exactly how and where each bone was found.

The Battle Over Sue

The trucks holding Sue's bones drove to a laboratory in South Dakota. Experts there spent months cleaning and studying Sue's bones. Their work, however, came to a sudden stop. Different people and groups claimed to own Sue. Among them were the owner of the land where the fossils were found and the U.S. government. FBI agents came and took the bones away.

Before the legal problems began, fossil experts started removing rock from around Sue's skull.

Tyrannosaurus Sue was now caught up in a legal battle. For five years, the battle dragged on. Finally Sue's fate was decided. The judge ruled that Sue belonged to the landowner. He was free to sell the bones if he wished.

Sue's case made headlines. TV newscasts and newspapers across the country reported on the battle over the bones.

Sue's bones were packed in boxes and stored while the trial dragged on.

Sue Is Sold

The landowner who had won the court fight decided to sell Sue at an **auction**. The event took place at Sotheby's, a fancy auction house in New York City. Sue's skull was put on display in a showroom. The rest of the bones were kept in a warehouse about 40 blocks away.

Sue's skull at the auction house

Many people came to the auction. Some were private collectors. Others were from museums. In less than ten minutes of **bidding**, the **gavel** came down. Sue had been bought by the Field Museum of Natural History in Chicago. Their winning bid was $7.6 million.

The Field Museum worked hard to raise money to bid on Sue. They received a lot of help from businesses, including the McDonald's Corporation and Walt Disney World Resorts.

SOTHEBYS
LOT 1 US$ 7600000

BR. POUND 4703640
FR. FRANC 45284600
GER MARK 13474800
LIRA '000' 13211460
YEN '000' 924160
SWISS FRANC 11054200
ALL CONVERSIONS APPROXIMATE

Including all the auction fees, the Field Museum paid a final price of $8.36 million for Sue. It was the highest price ever paid for a fossil.

Sue's New Home

The Field Museum turned out to be a perfect home for Sue. Fossil experts continued the work that had begun in South Dakota. Over the next two years, they finished cleaning the bones and the gigantic skull. They also made models of missing bones.

Huge banners outside the Field Museum announced Sue's arrival.

Visitors to the museum could look into the laboratory where Sue's bones were being cleaned.

Finally, it was time to put the skeleton together. Sue would have to take one more trip. This time the fossils were shipped to a giant art studio in New Jersey. A steel frame was built there. It held Sue's bones in place. Each bone could be removed so that scientists could study it up close.

Workers piece together Sue to prepare the skeleton for display.

Sue's skull was too heavy to be held up by a steel frame. The museum made a model of the skull that was light enough to be displayed on top of the skeleton.

Sue's Big Day

It was the morning of May 17, 2000. In the grand hall at Chicago's Field Museum, the music began. Spotlights and mist swirled. A curtain fell. Sue's fans were finally meeting the giant *T. rex*.

People from around the world came to the event. Among them was Susan Hendrickson.

Sue on opening day

"Seeing her standing there, this amazing creature that once walked our Earth, took my breath away," Susan later said.

Susan believed that the best thing about Sue was that the dinosaur would inspire people to learn more. Scientists at the museum agreed. Behind the scenes, they had spent more than two years learning about Sue.

Sue's skull is displayed in a glass case. Now visitors can come face-to-face with Sue.

Museum scientists decided to put Sue's skeleton in an action pose. The *T. rex* looks like it is moving forward and turning to check out something off to the side.

Getting to Know Sue

Sue's skeleton included kinds of *T. rex* bones that had never been found before. Scientists learned new facts about how *T. rex* looked and moved from them. By studying Sue's skull, they discovered that *T. rex* had a better sense of smell than they expected.

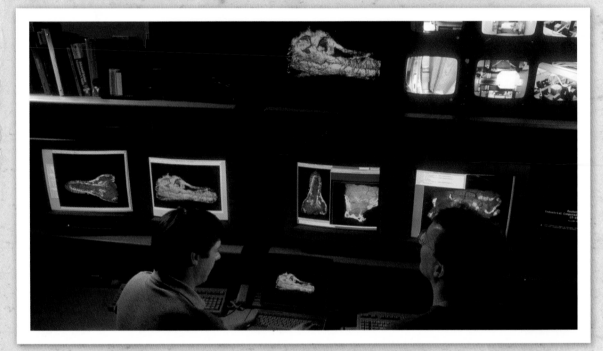

Scientists took high-tech CT scans of Sue's skull. To do so, they had to use a giant machine that was built to examine airplane engines.

Today, most scientists think that birds are the **descendants** of dinosaurs. Bones from Sue's skeleton gave them more evidence of the dinosaur-bird connection.

Many mysteries remain, however. How did *T. rex* use its tiny arms? Is Sue really a female? Did *T. rex* hunt live animals or feed on dead ones? Or did it get food both ways?

With questions like these still waiting to be answered, the work is far from done. *Tyrannosaurus* Sue's future might turn out to be as exciting as the dinosaur's past.

At the museum, *Tyrannosaurus* Sue towers over visitors just as the dinosaur once towered over other animals.

A Trip Back in Time: Who Lived with Sue?

Dinosaurs lived on Earth for around 150 million years. Scientists divide the time in which the dinosaurs lived into three periods—the Triassic period (250 to 205 million years ago), the Jurassic period (205 to 145 million years ago), and the Cretaceous period (145 to 65 million years ago).

T. rex lived near the end of the Cretaceous period. Here are three dinosaurs that lived at the same time and in the same places as *T. rex*.

Edmontosaurus

This plant-eater was one of the most common dinosaurs of its time—and probably one of *T. rex's* most common meals.

FACTS

Edmontosaurus
(ed-*mon*-toh-SOR-uhss)

- belonged to a group of dinosaurs known as the duckbills, because of their rounded, toothless beaks

- named for the Edmonton rock formation in western Canada, where its bones were first found

- **size:** 42 feet (13 m) long and 10 feet (3 m) high at the hips (about the same size as *T. rex*)

Triceratops

Like *Edmontosaurus*, this plant-eater often showed up on *T. rex*'s menu.

FACTS

Triceratops
(trye-SER-uh-*tops*)

- used its sharp horns as weapons to defend itself against attackers

- had a sharp beak that it used as a plant clipper when it ate

- **size:** 30 feet (9 m) long and 7 feet (2 m) high at the hips (smaller than *T. rex*)

Troodon

This meat-eater was faster and probably a lot smarter than *T. rex*. It was also much smaller and would make a quick getaway if *T. rex* came near.

FACTS

Troodon
(TROH-oh-don)

- name means "wounding tooth"

- had much better vision than *T. rex* and could probably see well at night

- **size:** 6–11 feet (2–3 m) long and 3 feet (1 m) high at the hips (about a quarter of the size of *T. rex*)

Glossary

amber (AM-bur)
a clear, yellowish, stone-like
fossil that forms from tree sap

ancient (AYN-shunt)
very old

auction (AWK-shuhn)
a sale where something is sold
to the person who offers the
highest price

badlands (BAD-landz)
an area with rocks that have
been sculpted into unusual
shapes by harsh winds and rain

bidding (BID-ing)
offering a certain amount of
money for something

burlap (BUR-lap)
a kind of heavy fabric

descendants (di-SEND-uhnts)
animals that come from a
family that lived earlier
in time

dig (DIG)
an exploration of a piece of land
where people dig for fossils

extinct (ek-STINGKT)
a kind of plant or animal that
has died out; when there are
no more alive on Earth

fiercest (FIHRSS-ist)
most dangerous

fossils (FOSS-uhlz)
what is left of plants or
animals that lived long ago

fragile (FRAJ-il)
easily broken

gavel (GAV-uhl)
a small hammer used by the
person in charge of an auction
to signal a completed sale

gender (JEN-dur)
being male or female

graveyards (GRAYV-yardz)
places where dead people or
animals are buried

plaster (PLASS-tur)
a mixture of water and tiny
bits of rock that hardens as
it dries

preserved (pri-ZURVD)
protected

sap (SAP)
a liquid that flows through
a plant and carries food and
nutrients

tombs (TOOMZ)
rooms, graves, or buildings in
which dead bodies are buried

tyrant (TYE-ruhnt)
a powerful and cruel ruler

Bibliography

Atkins, Jeannine. *How High Can We Climb? The Story of Women Explorers.* New York: Farrar, Straus and Giroux (2005).

Fiffer, Steve. *Tyrannosaurus Sue: The Extraordinary Saga of the Largest, Most Fought Over T. rex Ever Found.* New York: W. H. Freeman and Company (2000).

Horner, John R. *The Complete T. rex.* New York: Simon & Schuster (1993).

Larson, Peter, and Kristin Donnan. *Rex Appeal: The Amazing Story of Sue, the Dinosaur That Changed Science, the Law, and My Life.* Montpelier, VT: Invisible Cities Press (2002).

www.bhigr.com (Web site of the Black Hills Institute of Geological Research, Inc.)

Read More

Hendrickson, Sue (as told to Kimberly Weinberger). *Hunt for the Past: My Life as an Explorer.* New York: Scholastic (2001).

Horner, John R., and Don Lessem. *Digging Up Tyrannosaurus rex.* New York: Knopf Books for Young Readers (1992).

Larson, Peter, and Kristin Donnan. *Bones Rock! Everything You Need to Know to Be a Paleontologist.* Montpelier, VT: Invisible Cities Press (2004).

Relf, Pat, with the SUE Science Team of The Field Museum. *A Dinosaur Named Sue: The Story of the Colossal Fossil.* New York: Scholastic (2000).

Robinson, Fay, with the SUE Science Team of The Field Museum. *A Dinosaur Named Sue: The Find of the Century.* New York: Scholastic (1999).

Learn More Online

Visit these Web sites to learn more about Susan Hendrickson and the *T. rex* she discovered:

http://sue-hendrickson.net

http://teacher.scholastic.com/activities/dinosaurs/expert/transcript.htm

www.fieldmuseum.org/sue

Index

About the Author

Natalie Lunis has written more than two dozen science
and nature books for children. She hunts for fossils at the
American Museum of Natural History in New York City.